D1624167

100 Small Comforts

Wise and Witty Words to
Lift the Spirit

Illustrations by
Michael Woloschinow

Lawrence Teacher Books
Philadelphia

Mechanicals produced by book soup publishing, inc.

Cover and interior design by Susan Van Horn

Illustrations © 2001 by Michael Woloschinow

Quotes compiled by Christopher Hood
Edited by Mindy Brown

ISBN 1-930408-18-8

10 9 8 7 6 5 4 3 2 1

Please support your local book or gift store. However,
if you cannot find this book there, you may order it
directly from the publisher. Please add $1.50 for
postage and handling. Send check or money order to
the address below.

LAWRENCE TEACHER BOOKS
1 Pearl Buck Court
Bristol, PA 19007

INTRODUCTION

Every human being has the potential to reach for the stars—we sometimes just need a few words of encouragement.

This volume gathers a host of great thoughts that lift the spirit and comfort the soul. From them we gain the encouragement of the famous and the not-so-famous, the worldly and the wise. Read on, and uncover a small nugget of insight, an eloquent, shining moment of inspiration to remind you of the great possibilities we all carry within.

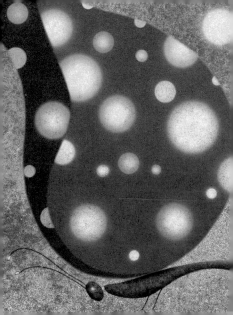

LIFE ISN'T ABOUT
FINDING YOURSELF—
LIFE IS ABOUT
CREATING YOURSELF.

GEORGE BERNARD SHAW,
Irish playwright (1856–1950)

Tomorrow is the most
important thing in life
. . . it puts itself in
our hands and hopes
we've learnt something
from yesterday.

JOHN WAYNE,
American actor (1907–1979)

If you can dream it,

you can do it.

WALT DISNEY,
American animation pioneer
(1901–1966)

LIFE IS EITHER A

DARING ADVENTURE,

OR NOTHING.

HELEN KELLER,
American writer, educator
(1880–1968)

What lies behind us
and what lies before
us are tiny matters
compared to what
lies within us.

- -

·OLIVER WENDELL HOLMES,
American jurist (1841–1935)

Goodness is the
only investment that
never fails.

HENRY DAVID THOREAU,
American writer (1817–1862)

10

KNOWLEDGE SPEAKS,

BUT WISDOM LISTENS.

JIMI HENDRIX,
American musician (1942–1970)

Be glad of life,
because it gives you
the chance to look
up at the stars.

- -

HENRY VAN DYKE,
American writer, educator,
clergyman (1852–1933)

The only way to discover the limits of the possible is to go beyond them to the impossible.

ARTHUR C. CLARKE,
British writer (b. 1917)

Not everything that
is faced can be changed,
but nothing can be
changed until it is faced.

- -

JAMES BALDWIN,
American writer (1924–1987)

EVERY EXIT IS AN
ENTRY SOMEWHERE.

TOM STOPPARD,
British playwright (b. 1937)

God not only plays
dice, he also
sometimes throws
the dice where they
cannot be seen.

STEPHEN HAWKING,
British physicist (b. 1942)

There is no such thing
in anyone's life as an
unimportant day.

ALEXANDER WOOLCOTT,
American writer (1887–1943)

PICK BATTLES BIG
ENOUGH TO MATTER,
SMALL ENOUGH TO WIN.

JONATHAN KOZOL,
21st century American writer

We so often look
so long and so regretfully
upon the closed door,
that we do not see the
ones which open for us.

ALEXANDER GRAHAM BELL,
American inventor (1847–1922)

TO LOVE ONESELF IS
THE BEGINNING OF A
LIFELONG ROMANCE.

OSCAR WILDE,
Irish playwright, poet, critic
(1854–1900)

There are only two ways
to live your life: One is
as though nothing is a
miracle, the other is as
if everything is.

ALBERT EINSTEIN,
German-born American physicist
(1879–1955)

23

I believe in God, only I
spell it Nature.

FRANK LLOYD WRIGHT,
American architect (1869–1959)

24

ALWAYS DO MORE THAN
IS REQUIRED OF YOU.

GEORGE S. PATTON,
American general (1885–1945)

Let us start a
new religion with
one commandment,
"Enjoy thyself."

ISRAEL ZANGWILL,
British playwright
(1864–1926)

I am always doing
things I can't do—that's
how I get to do them.

- -

PABLO PICASSO,
Spanish painter, sculptor (1881–1973)

No seed shall perish which the soul hath sown.

JOHN ADDINGTON SYMONDS,
British writer (1840–1893)

Whatever you can do or dream you can, begin it: Boldness has genius, power, and magic in it.

JOHANN WOLFGANG VON GOETHE,
German writer (1749–1832)

The golden
opportunity
you are seeking
is in yourself.

MARY ENGELBREIT,
21st century
American illustrator

IN THE DEPTHS OF
WINTER I FINALLY
LEARNED THERE
WAS IN ME AN
INVINCIBLE SUMMER.

ALBERT CAMUS,
French writer (1913–1960)

The best and most
beautiful things in the
world cannot be seen,
nor touched . . . but
are felt in the heart.

HELEN KELLER,
American writer, educator
(1880–1968)

WE MUST FOREVER
REALIZE THAT THE
TIME IS ALWAYS RIPE
TO DO RIGHT.

NELSON MANDELA,
South African leader, human
rights activist (b. 1918)

Happiness is
good health and
a bad memory.

INGRID BERGMAN,
Swedish actor (1915–1982)

The place to improve
the world is first in
one's own heart and
head and hands.

ROBERT M. PIRSIG,
American writer (b. 1928)

37

Age wrinkles
the body.
Quitting wrinkles
the soul.

DOUGLAS MACARTHUR,
American general
(1880–1964)

IT IS ONLY WITH THE HEART THAT ONE CAN SEE RIGHTLY.

ANTOINE DE SAINT-EXUPÉRY,
French aviator, writer
(1900–1944)

Who looks outside,
dreams. Who looks
inside, awakens.

CARL JUNG,
Swiss psychologist (1875–1961)

If you hear a voice
within you say, "you
cannot paint," then
by all means paint,
and that voice will
be silenced.

....

VINCENT VAN GOGH,
Dutch painter (1853–1890)

WE ARE NOT HUMAN
BEINGS ON A SPIRITUAL
JOURNEY; WE ARE
SPIRITUAL BEINGS ON
A HUMAN JOURNEY.

STEPHEN COVEY,
American leadership expert
(b. 1932)

Happiness is a how,
not a what; a talent,
not an object.

HERMANN HESSE,
German writer (1877–1962)

Happiness is the
spiritual experience
of living every
minute with love,
grace, and gratitude.

DENIS WAITLEY,
21st century American
psychologist

THERE IS NOTHING
THE BODY SUFFERS
THAT THE SOUL MAY
NOT PROFIT BY.

GEORGE MEREDITH,
British writer, poet (1828–1909)

The secret of health
for both body and
mind is to live in the
present moment wisely
and earnestly.

BUDDHA

If . . . we should cast the
gift of a loving thought
into the heart of a friend,
that would be giving as
the angels give.

GEORGE MACDONALD,
Scottish writer, poet (1824–1905)

ALTHOUGH THE WORLD
IS FULL OF SUFFERING,
IT IS ALSO FULL OF THE
OVERCOMING OF IT.

HELEN KELLER,
American writer, educator
(1880–1968)

Only those who will
risk going too far can
possibly find out how
far one can go.

·························

T. S. ELIOT,
British poet, critic (1888–1965)

What you are will
be yours forever.

HENRY VAN DYKE,
American writer, educator,
clergyman (1852–1933)

TO ACCOMPLISH GREAT
THINGS WE MUST
NOT ONLY PLAN BUT
ALSO BELIEVE.

ANATOLE FRANCE,
French writer (1844–1924)

To achieve the
impossible, it is
precisely the
unthinkable that
must be thought.

TOM ROBBINS,
American writer
(b. 1936)

Forget not that the
earth delights to feel
your bare feet and
the winds long to
play with your hair.

KAHLIL GIBRAN,
Lebanese poet, writer
(1883–1931)

IF YOU CANNOT BE

A POET, BE THE POEM.

DAVID CARRADINE,
American actor, director
(b. 1936)

Don't be afraid to

give up the good

for the great.

KENNY ROGERS,
American singer (b. 1938)

One hundred percent
of the shots you don't
take don't go in.

WAYNE GRETZKY,
Canadian ice hockey player
(b. 1961)

WHAT THE CATERPILLAR
CALLS THE END OF THE
WORLD, THE MASTER
CALLS A BUTTERFLY.

RICHARD BACH,
American writer (b. 1936)

Don't pray when
it rains if you
don't pray when
the sun shines.

------- -------

LEROY "SATCHEL" PAIGE,
American baseball player
(1906–1982)

Let your life lightly
dance on the edges
of time like dew on
the tip of a leaf.

RABINDRANATH TAGORE,
Indian poet, novelist,
philosopher (1861–1941)

OUR GREATNESS LIES

NOT SO MUCH IN

BEING ABLE TO REMAKE

THE WORLD . . .

AS IN BEING ABLE TO

REMAKE OURSELVES.

MOHANDAS K. GANDHI,
Indian political and
spiritual leader (1869–1948)

63

You are a child of
the Universe, no
less than the moon
and the stars.

MAX EHRMANN,
American writer (1872–1938)

Ideals are like the stars
...following them, you
will reach your destiny.

CARL SCHURZ,
American politician, journalist
(1829–1906)

THE FUTURE BELONGS
TO THOSE WHO BELIEVE
IN THE BEAUTY OF
THEIR DREAMS.

ELEANOR ROOSEVELT,
American first lady (1884-1962)

I believe in everything.

SHIRLEY MACLAINE,
American actor (b. 1934)

If all difficulties
were known at the onset
of a long journey,
most of us would never
start out at all.

DAN RATHER,
American television
anchor (b. 1931)

THERE WILL COME
A TIME WHEN YOU
BELIEVE EVERYTHING
IS FINISHED . . .
THAT WILL BE THE
BEGINNING.

LOUIS L'AMOUR,
American writer (1908–1988)

We can wait for
circumstances to make
up their minds, or
we can decide to act,
and in acting, live.

OMAR BRADLEY,
American general (1893–1981)

The human spirit is
never finished when
it is defeated . . .
it is finished when
it surrenders.

BEN STEIN,
American speechwriter,
television host (b. 1944)

WE MUST BE WILLING TO
LET GO OF THE LIFE WE
HAVE PLANNED SO AS TO
HAVE THE LIFE THAT IS
WAITING FOR US.

E. M. FORSTER,
British writer (1879–1970)

Faith is the daring

of the soul to

go farther than

it can see.

WILLIAM NEWTON CLARKE,
American clergyman
(1841–1912)

If you want
the rainbow, you
gotta put up
with the rain.

DOLLY PARTON,
American singer, actor
(b. 1946)

ONLY IF YOU HAVE
BEEN IN THE DEEPEST
VALLEY CAN YOU KNOW
HOW MAGNIFICENT
IT IS TO BE ON THE
HIGHEST MOUNTAIN.

RICHARD MILHOUS NIXON,
37th U.S. president (1913–1994)

Should you shield
the valleys from the
windstorms, you would
never see the beauty of
their canyons.

ELISABETH KÜBLER-ROSS,
American writer, psychiatrist (b. 1926)

78

Faith moves mountains,
but you have to
keep pushing while you
are praying.

MASON COOLEY,
American aphorist (b. 1927)

You must do the
thing you think you
cannot do.

- -

ELEANOR ROOSEVELT,
American first lady
(1884–1962)

Life is a promise;

fulfill it.

MOTHER TERESA,
Indian missionary,
humanitarian (1910–1997)

Whether you think
you can or think you
can't—you are right.

HENRY FORD,
American automobile pioneer
(1863–1947)

IT IS NOT BECAUSE
THINGS ARE DIFFICULT
THAT WE DO NOT DARE,
IT IS BECAUSE WE DO
NOT DARE THAT THEY
ARE DIFFICULT.

- -

SENECA,
Roman dramatist, philosopher
(3 B.C.E. – C.E. 65)

Dream as if you'll

live forever ... live as

if you'll die today.

JAMES DEAN,
American actor (1931–1955)

AFTER WINTER COMES
THE SUMMER. AFTER
NIGHT COMES THE DAWN.
AND AFTER EVERY
STORM, THERE COMES
CLEAR, OPEN SKIES.

SAMUEL RUTHERFORD,
Scottish clergyman (1600–1661)

Every action in our
lives touches on some
chord that will vibrate
in eternity.

EDWIN HUBBEL CHAPIN,
American clergyman (1814–1880)

HATE CANNOT DRIVE
OUT HATE; ONLY LOVE
CAN DO THAT.

DR. MARTIN LUTHER KING, JR.,
American civil rights leader
(1929–1968)

You must be the
change you wish to
see in the world.

MOHANDAS K. GANDHI,
Indian political and spiritual leader
(1869–1948)

THE SOUL IS NOT

WHERE IT LIVES,

BUT WHERE IT LOVES.

H. G. BOHN,
British publisher, bookseller
(1796–1884)

To be interested in the changing seasons is a happier state of mind than to be hopelessly in love with Spring.

GEORGE SANTAYANA,
Spanish-born American philosopher
(1863–1952)

If you run into a wall
...figure out how to
climb it, go through it,
or work around it.

MICHAEL JORDAN,
American basketball player (b. 1963)

When you get to the
end of your rope,
tie a knot and hang on.

-------------------------- --

FRANKLIN DELANO ROOSEVELT,
32d U.S. president (1882–1945)

TRY NOT TO BECOME
A MAN OF SUCCESS.
RATHER BECOME
A MAN OF VALUE.

ALBERT EINSTEIN,
German-born American
physicist (1879–1955)

It is better to deserve

honors and not have

them than to have them

and not deserve them.

------------- ----------------

MARK TWAIN,
American writer (1835–1910)

THINGS TURN OUT BEST
FOR PEOPLE WHO MAKE
THE BEST OUT OF THE WAY
THINGS TURN OUT.

JOHN WOODEN,
American basketball coach
(b. 1910)

Everybody can
be great: you only
need a heart full
of grace, a soul
generated by love.

DR. MARTIN LUTHER KING, JR.,
American civil rights leader
(1929–1968)

THE FRUIT OF SILENCE IS PRAYER, THE FRUIT OF PRAYER IS FAITH, THE FRUIT OF FAITH IS LOVE, THE FRUIT OF LOVE IS SERVICE, THE FRUIT OF SERVICE IS PEACE.

MOTHER TERESA,
Indian missionary, humanitarian
(1910–1997)

We carry within
us the wonders we
seek without us.

SIR THOMAS BROWNE,
British physician, writer
(1605–1682)

The one thing in
the world of value
is the active soul.

RALPH WALDO EMERSON,
American writer (1803–188?)

If you want to lift
yourself up, lift
up someone else.

BOOKER T. WASHINGTON,
American educator
(1856–1915)

NEVER LOOK DOWN ON ANYBODY UNLESS YOU'RE HELPING THEM UP.

JESSE JACKSON,
American civil rights leader,
politician (b. 1941)

How far you go in life
depends on your being
tender with the young,
compassionate with
the aged, sympathetic
with the striving
and tolerant of the

weak and the strong;
because someday in
life you will have
been all of these.

- -

GEORGE WASHINGTON CARVER,
American educator, botanist
(1864–1943)

From what we get,

we can make a living;

what we give, however,

makes a life.

ARTHUR ASHE,
American tennis player
(1943–1993)

If you want others
to be happy, practice
compassion; if you
want to be happy,
practice compassion.

THE 14TH DALAI LAMA,
Tibetan Buddhist leader
(b. 1935)

Let us be grateful
to people who
make us happy;
they are the
charming gardeners
who make our
souls blossom.

MARCEL PROUST
French writer (1871-1922)

The greatest good you
can do for another is
not just share your
riches, but reveal to
them their own.

BENJAMIN DISRAELI,
British politician, prime minister
(1804–1881)

WE ARE MORE THAN
WHAT WE DO ... MUCH
MORE THAN WHAT WE
ACCOMPLISH ... FAR
MORE THAN WHAT
WE POSSESS.

WILLIAM ARTHUR WARD
20th century American newspaper
writer, editor

There are only two
ways of spreading
light—to be the
candle or the mirror
that reflects it.

EDITH WHARTON,
American writer
(1862–1937)

Look at everything as though you were seeing it for either the first or last time . . . then your time on earth will be filled with glory.

BETTY SMITH,
American writer (1896–1972)

A ROCK PILE CEASES
TO BE A ROCK PILE THE
MOMENT A SINGLE
MAN CONTEMPLATES IT,
BEARING WITHIN HIM THE
IMAGE OF A CATHEDRAL.

ANTOINE DE SAINT-EXUPÉRY,
French aviator, writer (1900–1944)

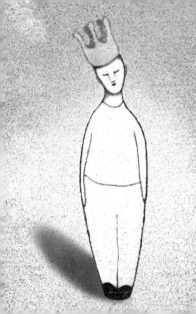

Do not go where
the path may lead,
go instead where
there is no path,
and leave a trail.

RALPH WALDO EMERSON,
American writer (1803–1882)

[To] take the first step in faith, you don't have to see the whole staircase: just take the first step.

DR. MARTIN LUTHER KING, JR.,
American civil rights leader
(1929–1968)

IN THE END, IT'S NOT
THE YEARS IN YOUR LIFE
THAT COUNT; IT'S THE
LIFE IN YOUR YEARS.

ABRAHAM LINCOLN,
16th U.S. president (1809–1865)